CONTENTS

CART-WHEELING
Wheels and Chariots
3

PEDAL PUSHING
Bicycles
6

EASY RIDING
Motorbikes and Engines
8

BUILT FOR COMFORT
Fuel and Cars
10

ROUGH RIDING
Off-road vehicles and Tyres
12

LOAD ON THE ROAD
Trucks
14

CATERPILLAR TRACKS
Machines at work
16

KEEPING ON TRACK
Trains
18

BUILT FOR SPEED
Racing cars
21

INDEX
Quiz answers
24

WALKER BOOKS
AND SUBSIDIARIES
LONDON • BOSTON • SYDNEY

MAKING TRACKS

Steve Parker

1 Life was a drag before wheels were invented. To move something very heavy like a large block of stone, you had to pull and slide your load along. It was backbreaking work.

2 Nobody knows who invented the wheel, or when. Some people believe it came from the turntable used by potters, and that one day someone thought — if I turn this on its side, it'll roll along!

3 Whatever happened, by 5,000 years ago people in Sumer (now southern Iraq) were building chariots with wheels that rolled around poles called axles. We know this from pictures on their tomb and temple walls. These also show us that the wheels were made from planks of wood.

4 It wasn't long before people discovered that light wheels roll more easily than heavy ones. So by 4,000 years ago, wheels were no longer solid — they were still made of wood, but they had spokes and a rim.

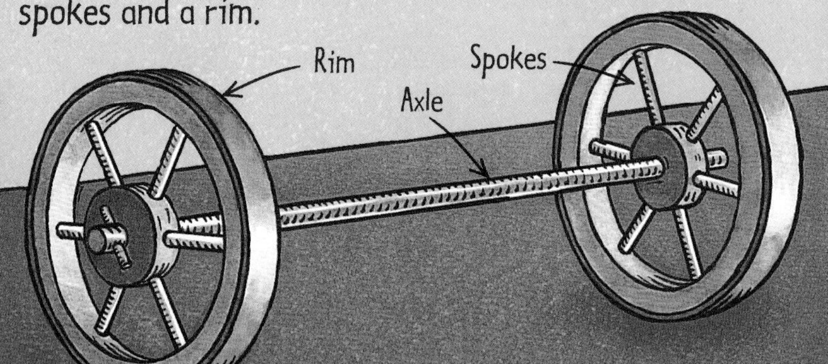

5 Thousands of years later, wheels are everywhere — we may not know who he or she was, but the bright spark who invented them changed our world for ever!

CART-WHEELING

1 This driver might look like he's taking things easy, but he's really hurtling around a racetrack at over 50 kilometres per hour!

2 He's driving a racing chariot called a sulky. Sulkies are designed to weigh as little as possible, because less weight means more speed.

3 To keep them light, sulkies are made from narrow pieces of metal and wood. Most of the metal pieces are hollow, which makes them even lighter.

4 People have been racing around in chariots for thousands of years. This one is called a biga, and it was used by the Romans over 2,000 years ago.

5 The biga was heavier and slower than a modern-day sulky, because it was made out of much thicker pieces of wood and metal.

6 Both the biga and the sulky have large wheels. But while the biga has one axle, the sulky has two — each wheel rolls around its own tiny axle.

7 Chariots are two-wheeled carts, and they're just one of the many kinds of cart that were used long ago.

8 Four-wheeled carts called wagons carried heavy loads like building stones or farmers' crops. Not all carts were pulled by horses, though — oxen, asses and other animals were also used.

9 Carts are still used in some countries today, of course. But in others, animal power has been overtaken by engine power since the first cars and trucks took to the roads in the 1880s.

PEDAL PUSHING

1 Believe it or not, the air slows us down! It pushes against us — and the faster we move, the harder it pushes.

2 That's why the wheels and frame of these track bikes are streamlined — with a sleek shape to help them slip smoothly through the air.

1 When bicycles were invented in the 1790s, they had no pedals, chains, gears or brakes. You pushed your feet along the ground to go, and dug your heels in to stop. It was another 50 years before pedals came along.

2 One of the oddest early bicycles was the penny-farthing, invented in 1870. Its huge front wheel made it difficult to climb up on to the seat — but very easy to fall off!

4 Streamlined track bikes like these can zip along at over 55 kilometres per hour — that's twice as fast as ordinary bikes go.

5 These superfast bikes are also superlight. They only weigh 8 kilos — half as much as a normal bike does.

3 The riders are streamlined, too. They're bending low over their bikes and wearing special helmets to make a smooth shape for the air to flow over.

6 Track bikes don't have brakes, but then they don't really need them. Racing cyclists don't usually stop — at least, not until they've crossed the finish line!

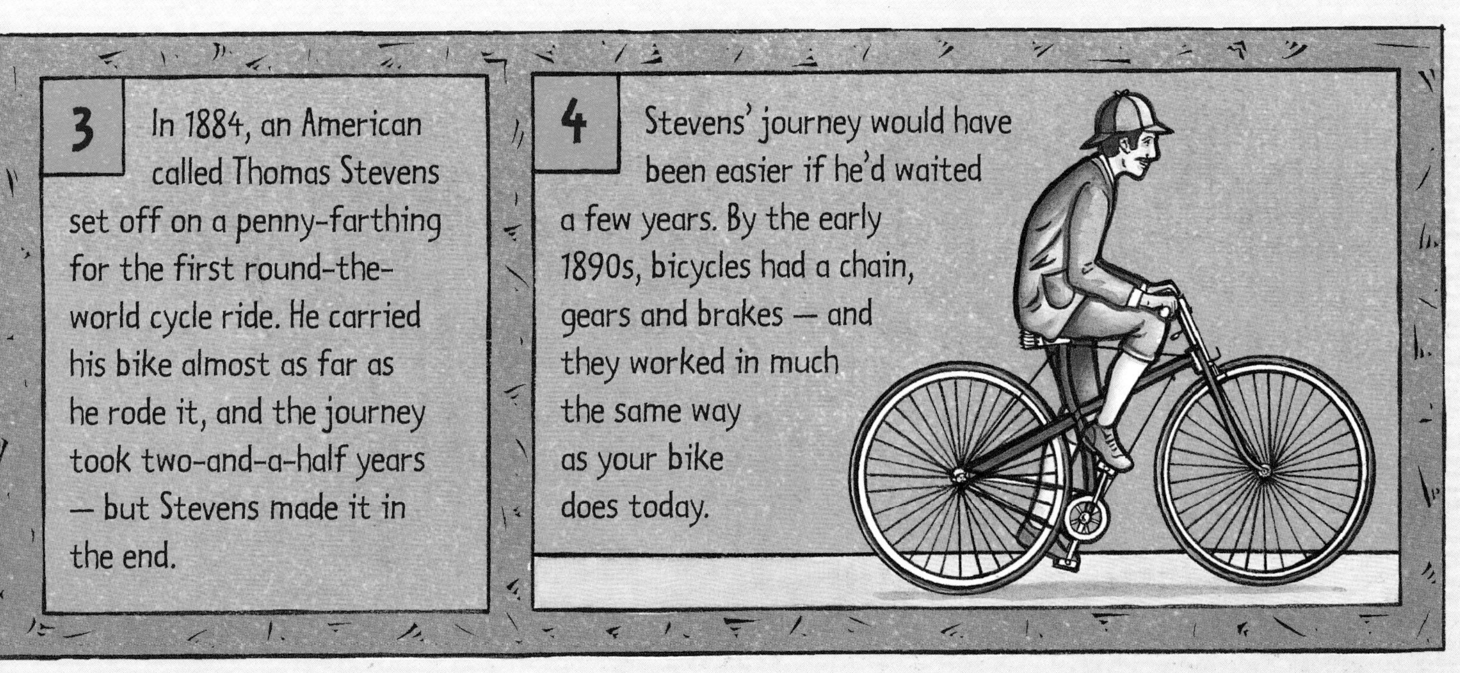

EASY RIDING

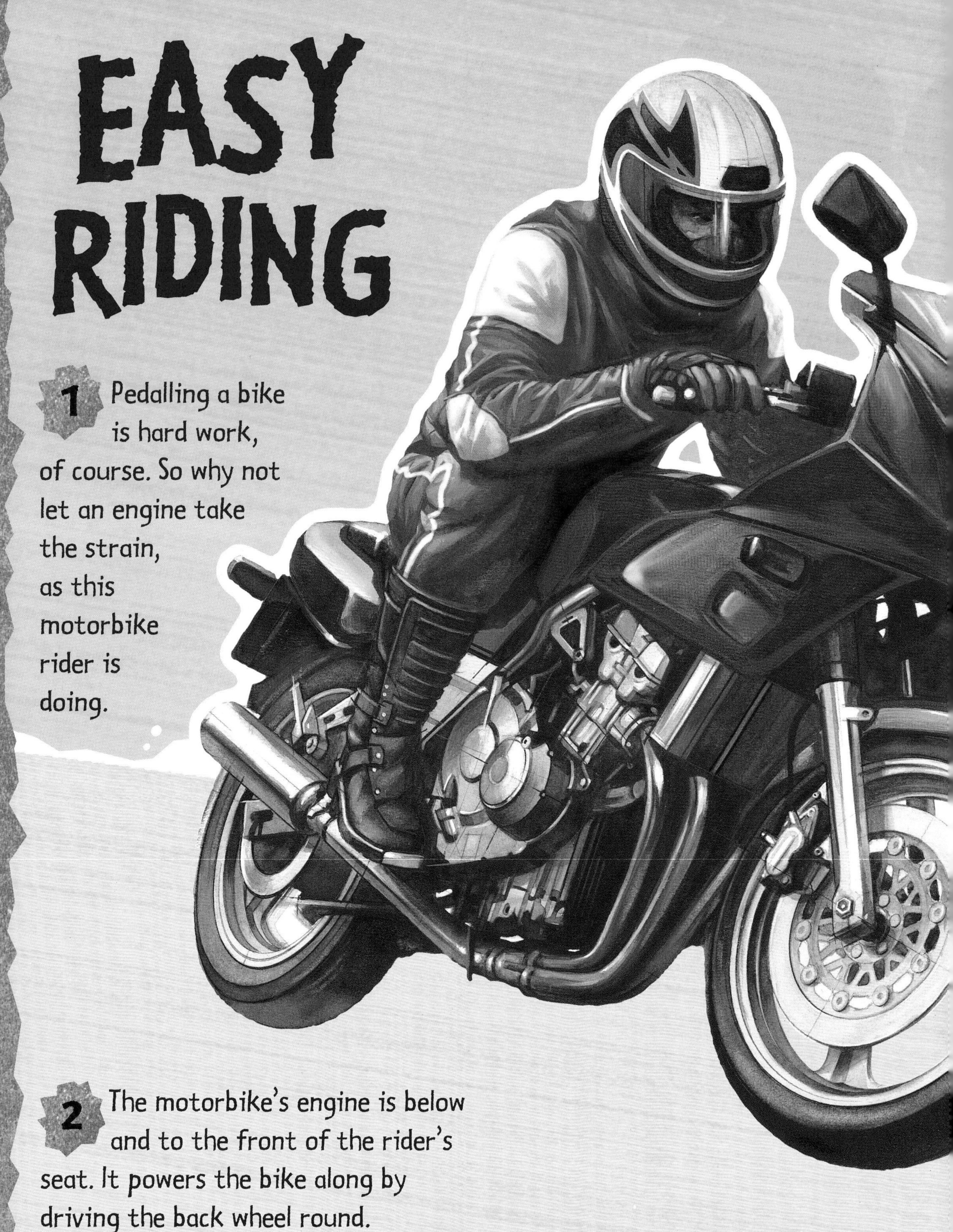

1 Pedalling a bike is hard work, of course. So why not let an engine take the strain, as this motorbike rider is doing.

2 The motorbike's engine is below and to the front of the rider's seat. It powers the bike along by driving the back wheel round.

3 But what powers the engine? Well, just like you, engines need energy to keep them going. You get your energy from the food you eat...

4 ...but a motorbike engine gets energy by burning petrol. The petrol tank is on top of the engine.

5 Having an engine means you won't run out of breath on a motorbike — watch out, though, you might run out of petrol!

1 How do petrol engines work? Inside the engine there are hollow chambers called cylinders, and inside each cylinder there's a piston.

2 Petrol and air are fed into each cylinder, then set alight by a spark of electricity to make them explode.

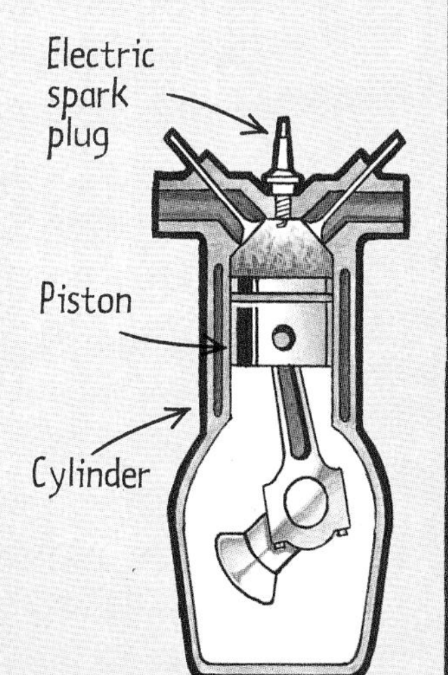

3

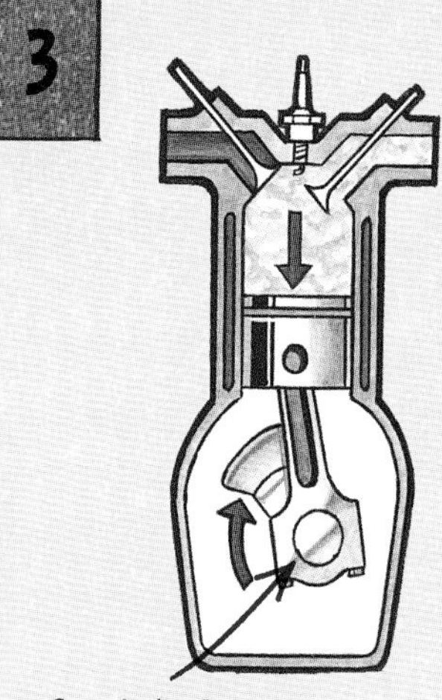

The explosion pushes the piston down. And as the piston goes down, it turns a part called the crankshaft.

4 This doesn't just happen once, though. There are dozens of explosions a second inside the cylinders — making all of the pistons whizz up and down, and turning the crankshaft round and round. And it's the spinning crankshaft that drives the wheels around.

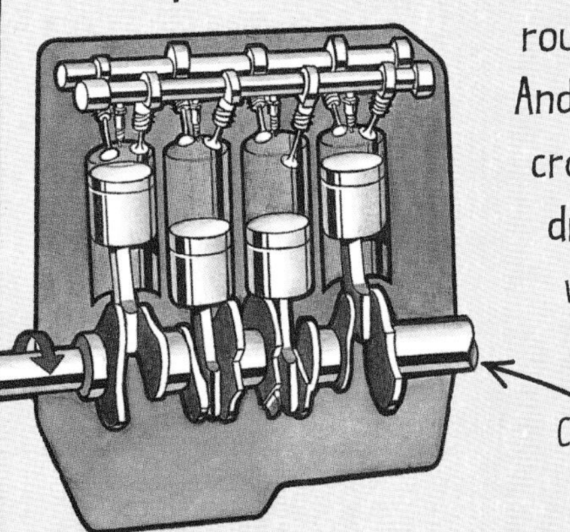

1 Most engines run on petrol or diesel, but these fuels are made from oil, and some time in the future the Earth's oil supplies will run out. Petrol and diesel also give off dirty exhaust fumes that pollute the air. That's why people are experimenting with different kinds of energy.

2 One bright idea is to use sunlight. Solar panels collect the Sun's energy and turn it into electricity to power a car — but you need to live in a very sunny place!

3 Batteries produce electricity too, of course, and you can recharge them when they run down. But to store enough electricity to power a car, the batteries need to be much bigger and heavier than the ones you use at home.

4 So the good news about electric cars is that they're quiet and fume-free. The bad news is that they only go half as far, half as fast, as petrol-powered cars!

1 Motorbikes are great for zipping about on, but cars can carry lots more people, in a lot more comfort — and protect them from the weather.

2 It's not really surprising then that cars are so popular. There are more than 4,000 million of them in the world.

BUILT FOR COMFORT

3 Cars come in all shapes and sizes, depending on what they're used for.

4 Sports cars are small and streamlined to help them go fast. While family cars are roomy, with space for a number of passengers.

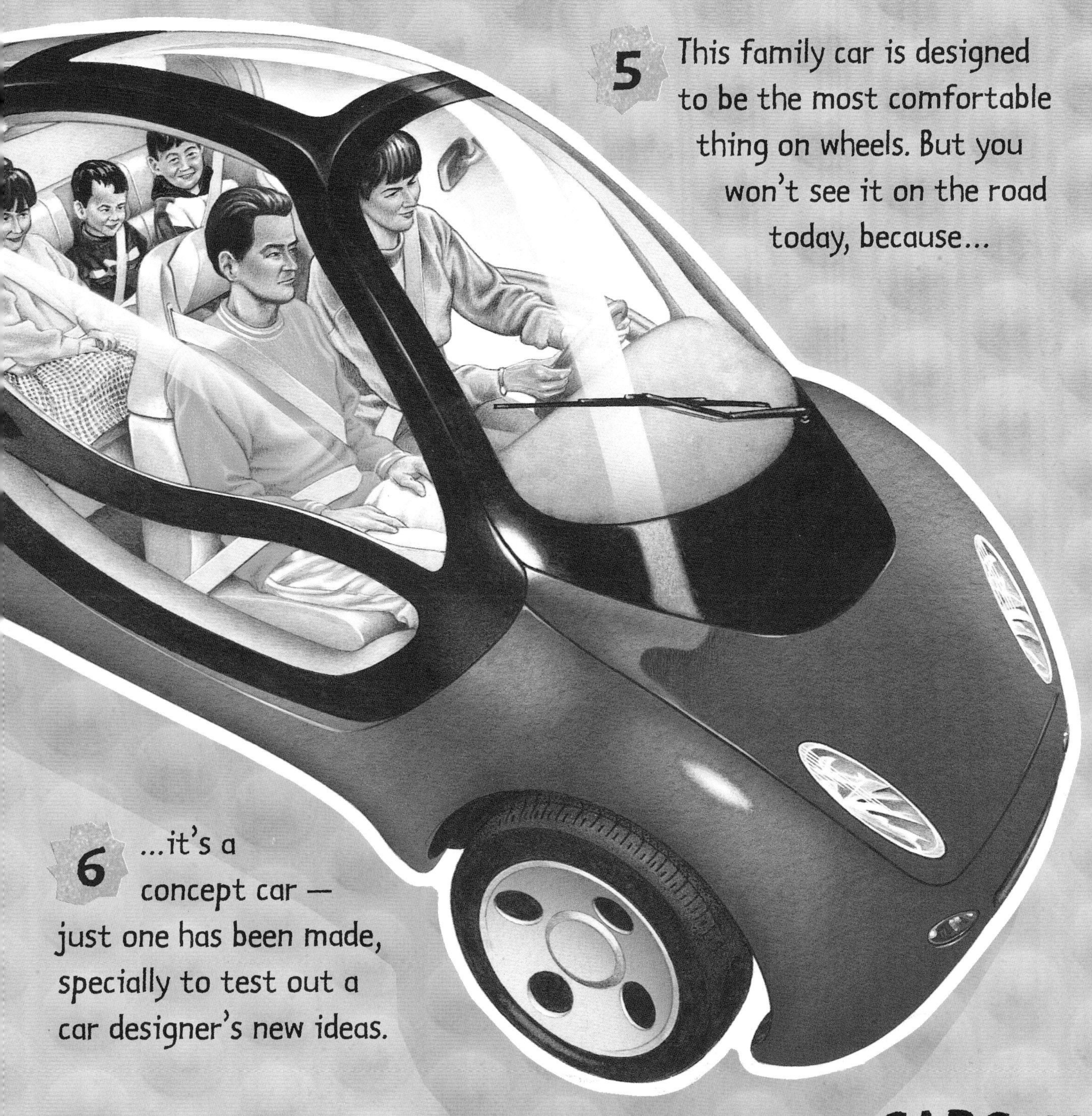

5 This family car is designed to be the most comfortable thing on wheels. But you won't see it on the road today, because...

6 ...it's a concept car — just one has been made, specially to test out a car designer's new ideas.

SOME CARS CAN TRAVEL ON WATER — TRUE OR FALSE?

ROUGH RIDING

1 The going gets tough when you're riding off smooth tarmac roads — so machines have to get tougher, too!

2 This is an ATV, an all-terrain vehicle. It's used on farms for jobs like rounding up sheep, and it has to cope with very rough ground.

3 In most cars, the engine just makes the back wheels turn round...

4 ...but in ATVs, it turns all four wheels. This is called four-wheel drive, and it helps off-road machines drive over slippery or soft surfaces like mud or sand.

TYRES ARE MADE FROM TREES — TRUE OR FALSE?

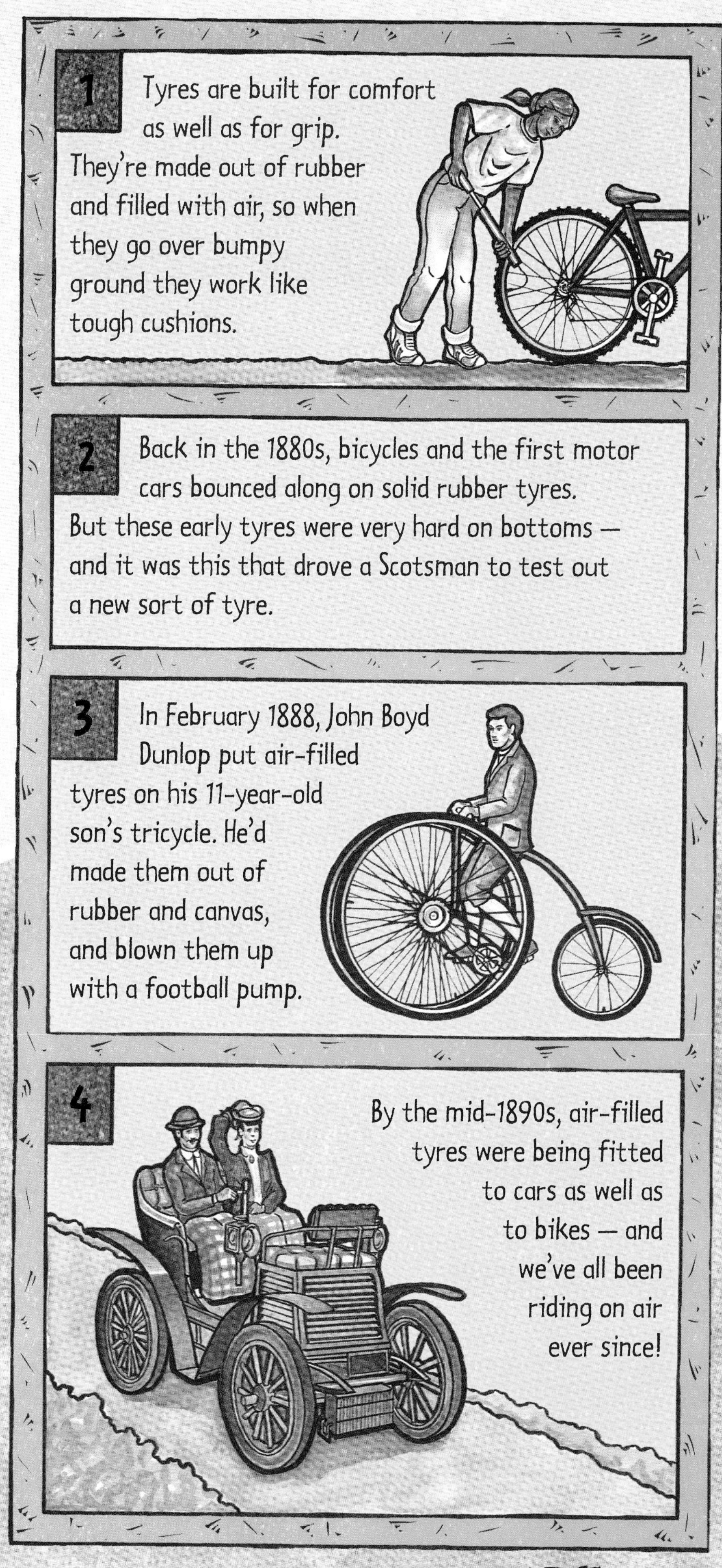

1 Tyres are built for comfort as well as for grip. They're made out of rubber and filled with air, so when they go over bumpy ground they work like tough cushions.

2 Back in the 1880s, bicycles and the first motor cars bounced along on solid rubber tyres. But these early tyres were very hard on bottoms – and it was this that drove a Scotsman to test out a new sort of tyre.

3 In February 1888, John Boyd Dunlop put air-filled tyres on his 11-year-old son's tricycle. He'd made them out of rubber and canvas, and blown them up with a football pump.

4 By the mid-1890s, air-filled tyres were being fitted to cars as well as to bikes – and we've all been riding on air ever since!

5 The ATV's big tyres give it extra grip. The pattern of grooves and ridges around a tyre is called tread, and on off-road tyres it's really chunky.

6 Tread works like the ridged soles on shoes – the lumpier and bumpier it is, the better it works on rough, wet or slippery ground.

LOAD ON THE ROAD

3 The other part, the trailer, is linked to the back of the tractor by a joint. This joint lets the truck "bend" when it drives around corners.

1 Big machines need big engines. And to pull its heavy load, this huge truck needs one that's five times more powerful than a car engine.

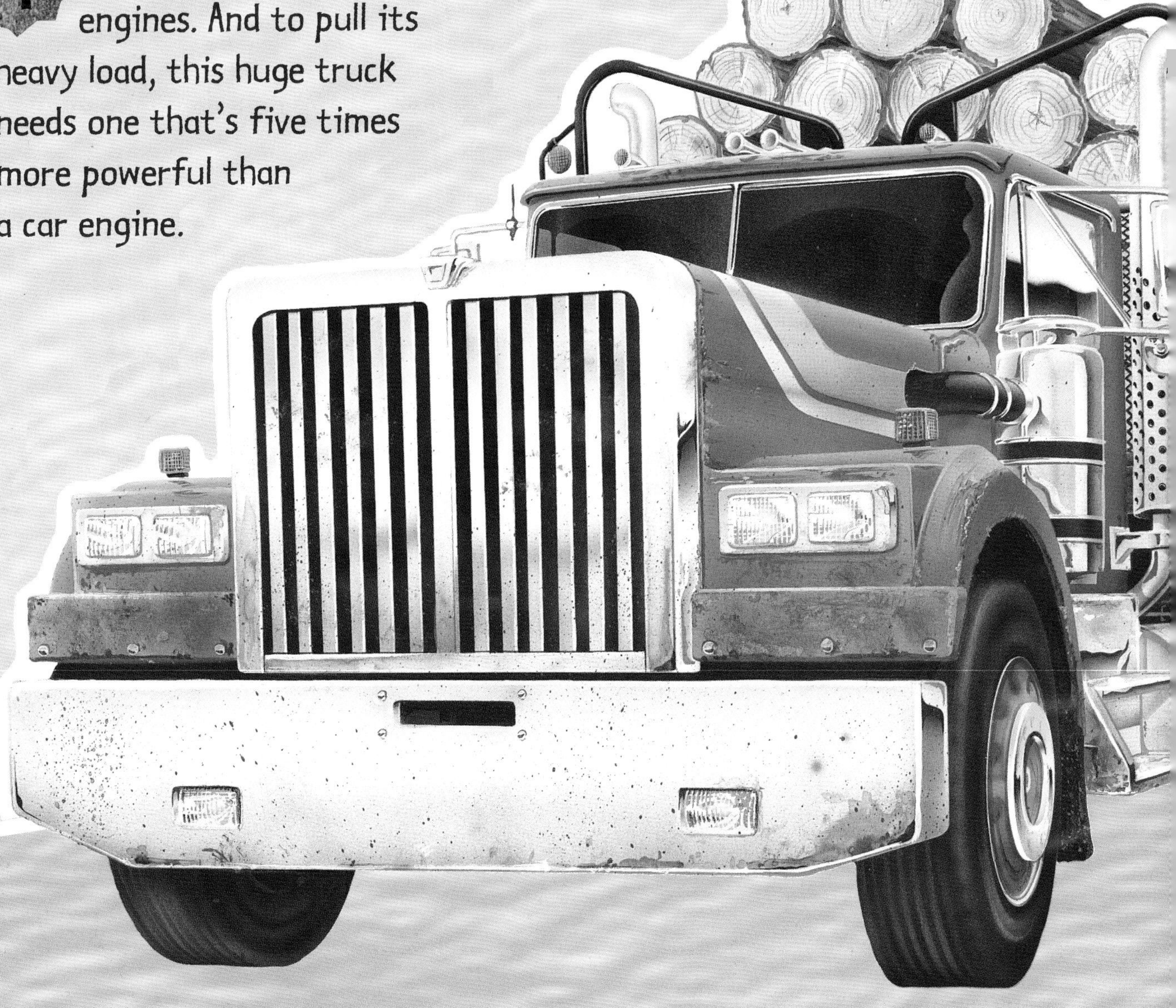

2 It's an articulated truck, made up of two jointed parts. In front there's a tractor unit, with the driver's cab and the engine.

TRUCKS CAN ONLY PULL ONE TRAILER — TRUE OR FALSE?

4 Trucks have diesel engines because they're more powerful than petrol ones. But truck engines are so big that they burn a massive amount of fuel.

5 And diesel gives off dirtier exhaust fumes than petrol does — so although it's great for power, it's worse for the air around us.

1 It's dawn, and while most of us are still asleep, a truck driver is getting ready for the day ahead. She checks there's enough fuel in the tank, and air in the tyres, then hitches her tractor unit to the trailer.

2 Out on the open road, she talks to other truck drivers on her CB (Citizens' Band) radio. Drivers use the CB to warn each other about accidents or traffic jams — or just to chat.

3 A few hours later the driver parks at a truck stop. She needs something to eat and the truck needs refuelling. After filling herself with a good meal, she puts 400 litres of diesel in her truck's fuel tank — that's almost ten times more than a family car holds.

4

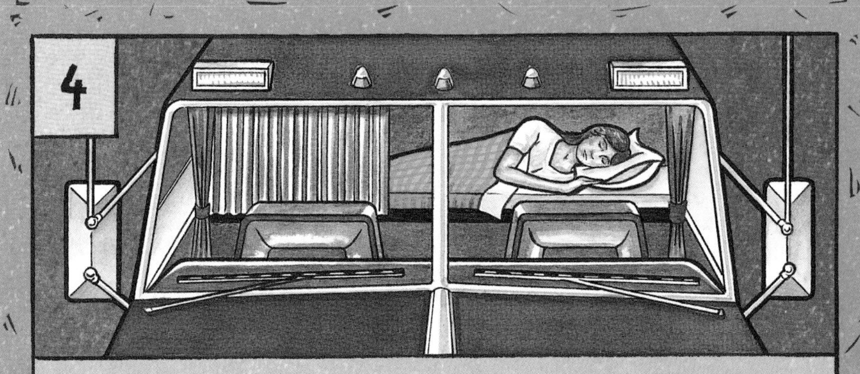

When evening comes there's no need to hunt for a hotel. At the back of the cab there's a bed, washbasin, cupboard and even a TV. The truck driver will be up at dawn again tomorrow, so it's early to bed. Good night!

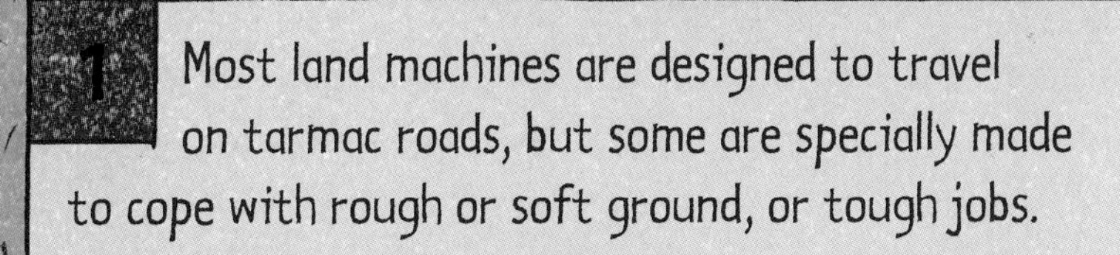

1 Most land machines are designed to travel on tarmac roads, but some are specially made to cope with rough or soft ground, or tough jobs.

2 To spread their weight and keep them from sinking into soft snow, snowmobiles have skis at the front and a wide caterpillar track at the back.

3 This machine is for harvesting grapes, and its high body and wide-apart wheels let it ride over grape vines without damaging them. Conveyor belts carry the grapes along the harvester's arm into the tractor's big bin.

4

Here's a log-collecting machine with legs and feet! Wheels or caterpillar tracks would trample young forest trees, but this machine can tiptoe carefully around them.

1 Building sites use really tough machines, and here's one that's designed never to get bogged down by work — a bulldozer.

2 To cope with shoving big loads about, bulldozers need to be heavy — this one weighs around 10 tonnes.

CATERPILLAR TRACKS

3 But even though it's so heavy, the bulldozer doesn't get stuck in soft sand or sticky mud.

4 That's because its weight isn't just pressing down on four tyres. Instead, it's spread along the whole length of two large caterpillar tracks.

5 A bulldozer gets its pushing power from a big diesel engine. In just one hour it can move more rubble than 100 people using shovels!

KEEPING ON TRACK

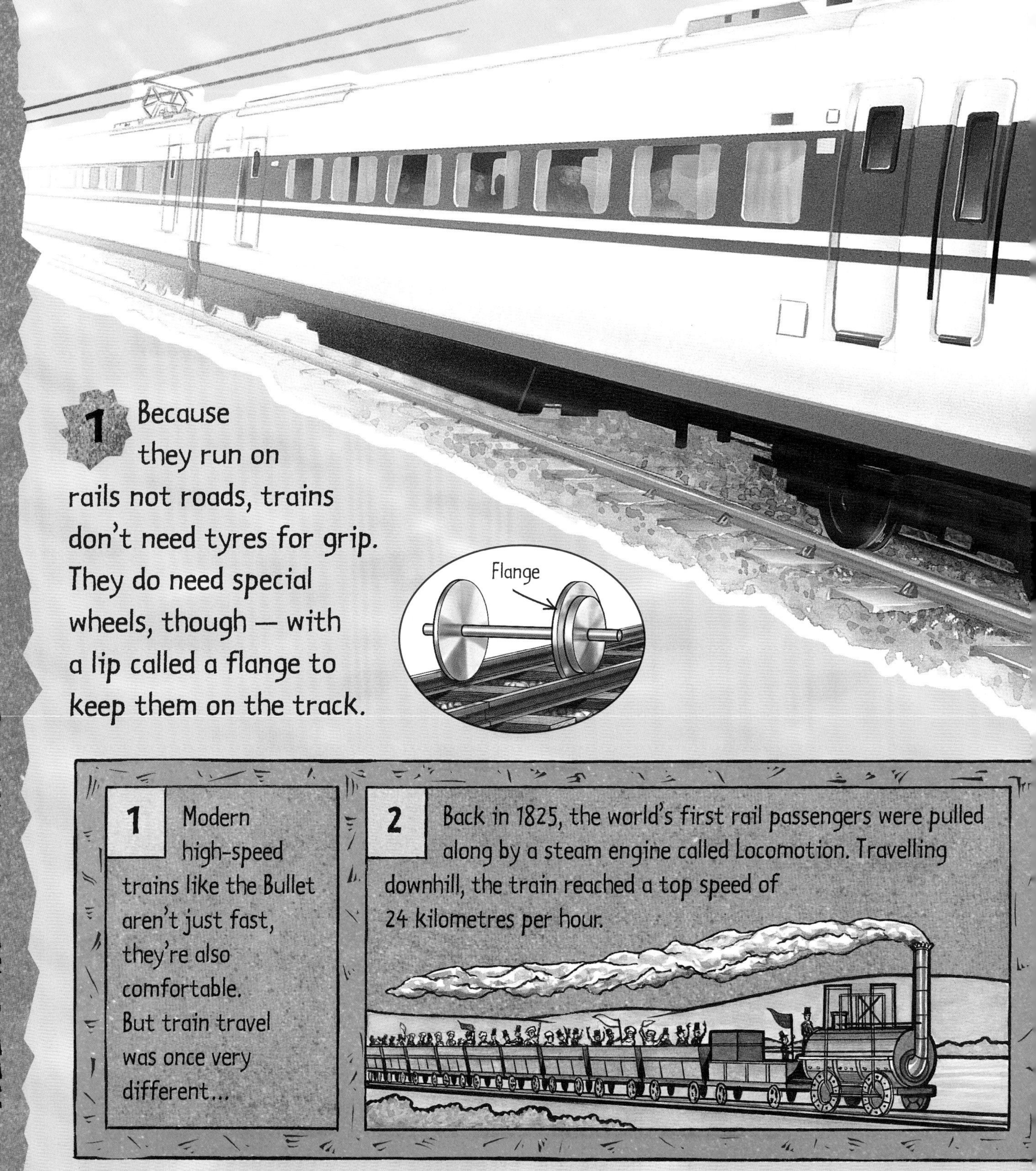

1 Because they run on rails not roads, trains don't need tyres for grip. They do need special wheels, though — with a lip called a flange to keep them on the track.

1 Modern high-speed trains like the Bullet aren't just fast, they're also comfortable. But train travel was once very different...

2 Back in 1825, the world's first rail passengers were pulled along by a steam engine called Locomotion. Travelling downhill, the train reached a top speed of 24 kilometres per hour.

2 This Japanese train is one of the fastest in the world. It's called the Bullet Train, and it flashes along the track at over 250 kilometres per hour.

3 The Bullet is an electric train. On its roof it has special connectors called pantographs, which feed electricity from overhead cables to its motors.

4 Most high-speed trains are pulled by the motors in their locomotive. But not this one. The Bullet's carriages have their own motors — so it isn't just pulled along, it's pushed as well!

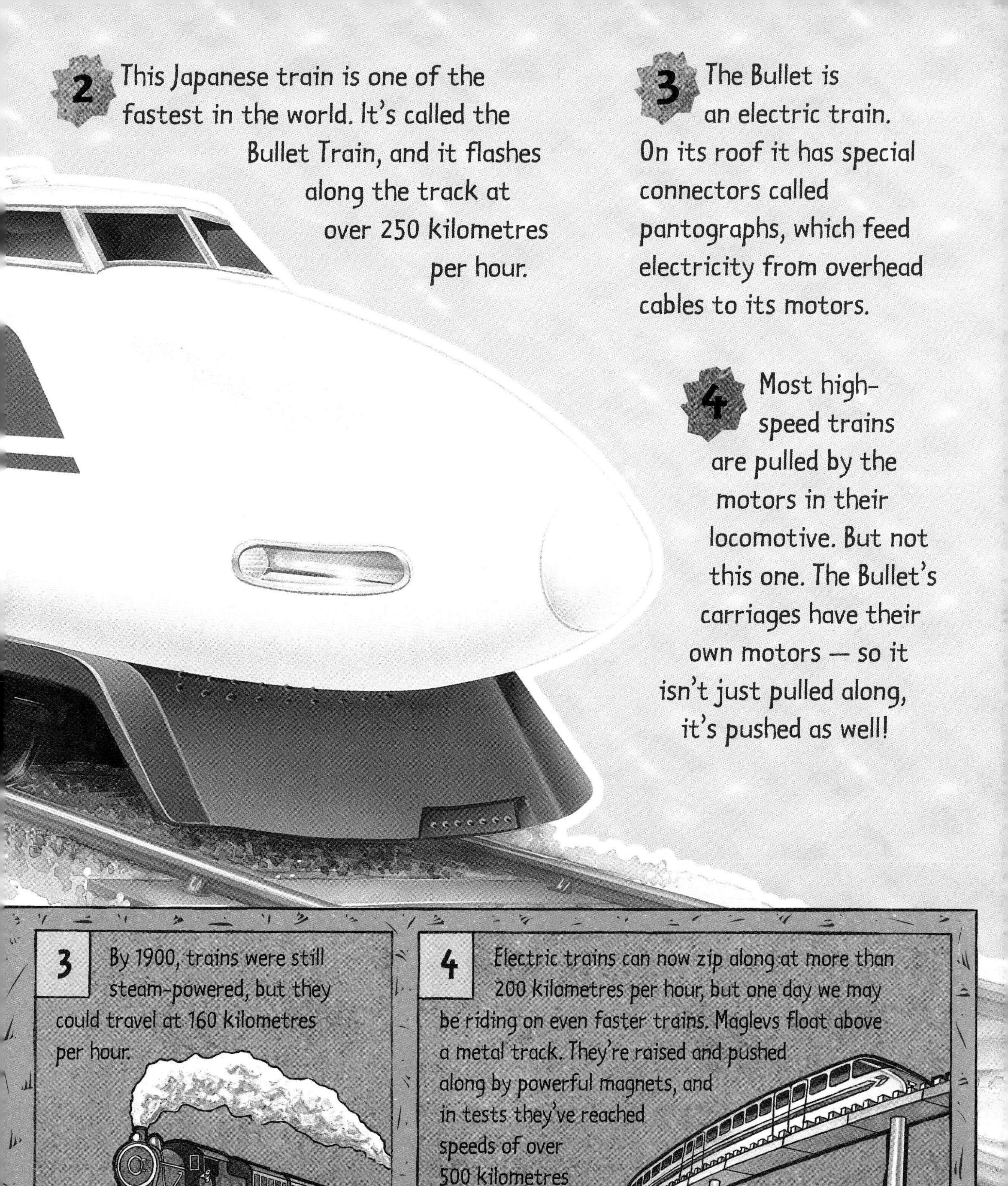

3 By 1900, trains were still steam-powered, but they could travel at 160 kilometres per hour.

4 Electric trains can now zip along at more than 200 kilometres per hour, but one day we may be riding on even faster trains. Maglevs float above a metal track. They're raised and pushed along by powerful magnets, and in tests they've reached speeds of over 500 kilometres per hour!

1 A Grand Prix race is about to begin. The F1 cars are in position on the start lines, called the grid, waiting for the off-signal.

2 The green start-light shows, and they're off! With a scream of noise from their engines, the cars race down the track towards the first bend.

3 Screech — CRUNCH — a car skids off into the barrier! Race organizers, fire officers and ambulance crew all rush over to help.

4 When fuel gets low or tyres wear down, the drivers pull off the track into the pits — a slip road with garages and workshops. It takes a team of mechanics less than 10 seconds to refuel a car and change all four wheels and tyres.

5 The crowd cheers as the chequered flag waves the winner across the finish line. The winning driver and team collect their prize, then it's time to pack. They're off to another track in another country — for the next race!

BUILT FOR SPEED

1 This Formula One (F1) car is one of the world's fastest road machines. Its powerful engine can take it to speeds of over 330 kilometres per hour.

2 Everything about this car is built for speed. It's so low and streamlined that the driver has to lie down inside it.

3 Every F1 car is built specially for its particular driver. Even the seats are designed to fit the exact shape of the driver's body.

4 F1 cars are only driven in Grand Prix races — the words grand prix are French for "great prize".

5 These cars are even zippier than F1 racers. They're called dragsters, and they're the fastest kind of racing car.

6 Dragsters power along at over 500 kilometres per hour. They use very short tracks, though, and drag races often last less than 5 seconds.

7 At speeds like this, normal brakes take too long to stop a car, so dragsters get a little extra help.

8 As the car hurtles over the finish line, the driver pulls a special lever — and whuummppp, a parachute shoots out and helps to slow the car down!

F1 tracks can be up to 3.5 kilometres long, and they have lots of curves and bends. About 20 cars race each other over a number of laps.

Drag tracks are straight and only 400 metres long. Just two cars race at a time.

INDEX

articulated truck 14
ATV (all-terrain vehicle) 12-13
axle 2, 4

battery 10
bicycle 6-7
bulldozer 16-17
Bullet Train 18-19

car 10-11, 13, 20-23
cart 5
caterpillar tracks 16, 17
chariot 2-5
concept car 11

diesel 10, 15
dragster 22-23

engine 5, 8, 9, 14, 15
electric car 10
electric train 19

Formula One car 20, 21
four-wheel drive 12
fuel 9, 10, 15

maglev 19
motorbike 8-9

off-road vehicle 12-13

petrol 9, 10
pollution 10

racing 3, 7, 20-23

snowmobile 16
streamlining 6, 7

train 18-19
tread, tyre 13
truck 14-15
tyres 13

wheel 2, 5, 12, 18

Main illustrations by Christian Hook (3, 4-5); Mike Lister (title page, 8-9, 12-13, 16-17); Lee Montgomery (6-7, 10-11); Richard Morris (cover, 14-15, 18-19); Darren Pattenden (20, 22-23).
Inset illustrations by Bob Holder. Picture-strip illustrations by Ian Thompson.

Thanks to Beehive Illustration, Hardlines, Helicopter Graphix.

Designed by Jonathan Hair and Matthew Lilly, and edited by Jackie Gaff and Paul Harrison.

First published 1997 by Walker Books Ltd, 87 Vauxhall Walk, London SE11 5HJ

This edition published 1998

2 4 6 8 10 9 7 5 3 1

This book has been typeset in Kosmik.

Printed in Hong Kong

British Library Cataloguing in Publication Data
A catalogue record for this book is available from the British Library.

ISBN 0-7445-5413-6

QUIZ ANSWERS

Page 2 — FALSE

Chariot races first took place over 2,300 years ago, in Ancient Greece.

Page 6 — TRUE

Bicycles always have two wheels — "bi" means two. A cycle with one wheel is called a unicycle.

Page 8 — FALSE

The world's fastest motorbike can reach nearly 520 km/h, but the fastest cars have rocket engines and speed along at more than 1,000 km/h.

Page 11 — TRUE

Some cars and trucks are specially designed to travel on water as well as on land. They're called amphibious vehicles.

Page 12 — TRUE

The rubber parts of a tyre are made from the sap of rubber trees.

Page 14 — FALSE

Road trains are trucks that pull two, three, and even four trailers at once.

Page 17 — TRUE

The world's biggest land vehicle, the Marion Crawler, has eight caterpillar tracks. It's used to carry the USA's space shuttles to their launch pad.

Page 18 — FALSE

Some trains, called monorails, ride on a single track which runs under, or above, the middle of the train.

Page 20 — TRUE

Warm tyres grip better than cold ones, so F1 tyres are wrapped in electric blankets before a race, to heat them.